Mind Music

C.N. CANTELON

Order this book online at www.trafford.com
or email orders@trafford.com

Most Trafford titles are also available at major online book retailers.

Print information available on the last page.

ISBN: 978-1-6987-1384-7 (sc)
ISBN: 978-1-6987-1382-3 (hc)
ISBN: 978-1-6987-1383-0 (e)

Library of Congress Control Number: 2023900201

Trafford rev. 01/05/2023

 www.trafford.com
North America & international
toll-free: 844-688-6899 (USA & Canada)
fax: 812 355 4082

Contents

A Man Stands 1

As Shadows Drift 2

Catacombs 3

Cold Air 4

Do You Not See 5

Everyone Has Fears 7

Fear 8

Gnats 9

I Do Not Wish 11

In Thought 12

Locked In 14

Love for You 15

Love Is 16

Love Time 18

Love, Like The Tide 19

Love's Reality 20

Now Time 21

Place 22

Poetry Is 23

Rhyming Day 24

She is An Angel 25

Spring Fall 26

Stafford 27

Sun Reflects 29

The Bridge 30

The Spring Has Come 32

Thoughts 33

Walking through Woods 34

We Are Free 36

We Walk Along 37

What's Right 38

When We Give Words 39

Prism 40

A Man Stands

A man stands at a bus stop,
Leaning against the pole,
One leg crossed before the other
And both hands cupped to his mouth.
What does this say about him?
Why do I care?
All day long, I observe
People in assorted places
But we never meet.
So, I create their lives
To suit my preconceptions.
Am I right?
Does it even matter?
Do other people use me
In such a selfish way?
If so, what would I like to say?

*

Here's something I wrote 7-12-2001:

As Shadows Drift

As shadows drift across the day
And secrets find the light,
Our hope rests in the simple way
We try to do what's right.
No promise holds us in contempt.
We act as though new born.
Though worldly cares may tease and tempt,
We look on them with scorn.
For we have found a treasure trove
Too real to be ignored.
Based in humility and love,
It lives, our eternal reward.

*

Catacombs

Here we hovel in the catacombs of our fears,
Relying on doubt and distrust above our faith.
We dare not face the light of day, as it appears
In the form of a dastardly wraith!
Our churches and markets are closed.
Our selfish desires are disclosed.

*

Cold Air

The air was cold,
But the temperature didn't matter.
Cold air is still breathable.
We shared a place in time
And a moment in a dimension of existence
Which only mattered because we were then and there.
I carry such a kind memory
Within my soul, and though
You are not here with me,
You have become part of me.
I will never exist without you.

*

Do You Not See

Do you not see how your every thought
engenders mystery?
How your every action causes ripples
in the fabric of our lives?
How your every word reverberates
in the caverns of our hearts?
You are the essence of the universe,
and no less a god than the highest mountain
or the deepest sea.
Yet, you do not see this?
Sound abounds in me,
but no words issue from these lips.
Truth echoes through the hollowness
of empty expectations,
yielding naught but dust
and coats of rust
on the secret ores of our hopes.
You sell yourself short.
No, you are not the center of the universe,
but the universe is no less centered in you
than in the greatest galaxy of our wonders.

What you do or say has weight.
Assure eternity that this matters to you
and eternity will ever remember this day
and you.
Repeat this to yourself
each moment of every day,
and you will be an angel in our hearts.

*

Everyone Has Fears

Everyone has fears.
We are not defined by our fears,
But by those moments in which
We find the courage to face them
And to do what's right,
In spite of the onsequences.
Do not fear the consequences of courage.
They are preferrable to those of fear.

*

Fear

Always, there will be injustice,
Born of fear - born in prejudice
And jealousy. But we need not be
The servants of these fears,
Nor the bearers of their injustices.
We are free to rise above them
And embrace our dreams -
Free to share our love with all
Whom we meet on the path we walk.

*

Gnats

Gnats, this morning,
Rising from the steps -
Moss-covered, damp estuary -
On my constitutional;
I woke the lugubrious beasts.
Gnats of resentment
For my insolence,
They rose to the assault.
I trudged on
Throughout the angry realization
That the relationship
Could not be with myself.
Clouds of battle
Lowered upon the field
While I, who long demured
Before their angry call,
Stood firm to face
All past remonstrance
And own my part.

No longer do I hide.
No more will I deny
Their horrors
As my time slips by.
I trudged on
Through the angry mob,
Aware but unconcerned.
What gnats we are
As Nature passes through us.

*

I Do Not Wish

I do not wish to waste your time.
Nobody wasted any of mine.
But, I will share a thought or two.
Do with them whatever you wish to do.
I take each moment, first and last,
As the door to my future and gate to my past.
For all I really have is now.
I must employ it and enjoy it, somehow.

*

In Thought

I sit in thought.
Was I, one time, taught?
What poetry is mine?
I write which words flow through me,
Unconscious of meter or rhyme.
Does that animate the muse?
Has Erato my tongue,
Or merely my ear?
Is it lingual or audial
That I write?
Do I speak
Or merely write what the mind may hear?
It is of no great consequence.
The meter or the rhyme
Is neither history's
Nor original and, therefore, mine.
All words and thoughts -
All sounds and heartbeats

Exist strictly within the audience
And all within this moment of time.
A poem is real, only, when beheld
By the eyes or ears of the reader.

*

Locked In

Locked in ourselves, we wander
Down avenues of dubious destinations.
We question every stone, and ponder
Each memory of once-reliant personal relations.
Who were these souls
And where did they go?
We examine their prior roles
And wonder, who did we really know?

*

Love for You

How can I tell you what these past few years have meant to me?
Without you, I wouldn't be alive, obviously.
But, more than that, you have brought out the good
And showed me I can do things I never thought I could,
And do them joyfully, grateful for the opportunity
To make you happy and make you proud of me.
I know I'm blessed to have you in my life.
I'm more grateful than you know to have you as my wife.
Still, I'm aware of how far I have, still, to go
And the myriad ways in which I need to grow.
But I have faith that, with you by my side,
I will progress and you will be my guide.
I love you more than I could ever tell,
And I can talk, as you know all too well.
But, if my deeds can speak louder than words,
Let my love soar on the wings of a thousand birds
That you might feel the rush of its passing wind
And know a love that time can never rescind.

*

Love Is

Love is a form of insanity.
Tell me, what else can it be?
When all I think about is you –
What you like –
What you think –
What you do….
Love is the bane of humanity.
It warps us with pride and with vanity,
As we try to appear as we're not –
Someone cool –
Someone sweet –
Someone hot!
So, tell me, how can it be?
I love you!
You love me!
Love has taken control, again,
Driving me –
Driving you –
Driving both of us insane!

Help me find the secret door
That can lead me to
A place where love is true,
So we can love one another, more and more.

*

Love Time

When we share love,
It isn't a feeling in time and space.
Love seems to exist forever and everywhere.
Therefore, we never lose those we love.
They are with us always,
As we are with them.

*

Love, Like The Tide

Love, like the tide, is an ebb and flow,
Always rushing inside,
But with nowhere to go.
It carresses our hearts
As tide washes the sand;
Ever changing in parts;
Always ready at hand.

*

Love's Reality

I did not expect you to love me.
I knew you were difficult.
So, I was taking a risk
In commitment.
Still, I took the chance
And, in response,
You let me love you
And, in turn, you loved me.
All the rest,
The good and the bad,
Is our shared history.
Now, all I can ask
Is that you accept
The whole of me.
In return, I promise
To do my best
And be grateful
For all you give to me.

*

Now Time

Sun reflects on green leaves.
Reminds me Spring is here.
What eggs the seasonal bird conceives
Will, doubtless, soon appear,
And all the seeds
The new nest needs
Will fill the mother's craw,
While the father drives his foes away,
Lest eggs become their cowardly prey
Before the how of birth arrives.
And so, each year is like the last
And life gives future to the past.

*

Place

Where is my place
In this human race?
Why am I trying
To live before dying?
Perhaps, I am here
Just to make fun of fear!
If I should laugh out loud,
Would it worry the crowd?
That sounds kind of creepy....
I suspect I've grown sleepy.
Never mind. I am gone.
It's your turn. Carry on.

*

Poetry Is

Poetry is the conveyance of feeling.
It should not be so entwined as to be unintelligible.
Yet, it should not be so straight forward as to be plain.
Therefore, the poet listens to the wind before writing.
The wind, then, may caress the poet's pen
To render it sensitive, but sensible.

*

Rhyming Day

It's a rhyming day.
Sorry, I just woke up this way.
I'll probably pass the whole day away
With nothing meaningful to say,
But said, instead, in such a way
As to cause your inner music to play.

*

She is An Angel

She basks in the sunlight of her own soul.
Her kindness brings a warmth which glows,
Reflecting off surrounding personalities
In such a way as to draw out
From them their own auras,
Proving life both draws from heat
And offers its own emissions of warmth,
Either from friction or from comfort.
So, she touches all who meet her
And leaves them better for it.

*

Spring Fall

It is Spring.
Rain is expected,
But sunshine, too, should come.
This thing –
This pain I've resurrected –
Is only mine,
And I succumb
To the rain and the pain,
While the sunshine
Refuses to be mine.
Less than wise,
I realize
That all my dreams
And egotistical schemes
Are permanently on hold.
My story,
Never will be told.

*

Stafford

A walk outside to rehabilitate
Such vagaries as may exist
Within a mind bound in a state
Of self, expecting to resist
What others offer as purpose for the day.
Doing what we must, and what we may,
We dare the woods,
No doubt, with gratitude
For all its ills as well as goods,
Allowing us our latitude.
So, we stumble through the roots,
Stubbing our toes and cutting our boots.
Finally, we discover
A path we can employ
Which will, doubtless, lead to another
In which we may suffer and enjoy
Both what we do not wish to realize
As well as that we want to finalize.

Now, we turn, again, to Time's resolve.
We cannot delay life, anymore.
Whatever, we must, now, involve
Ourselves as tools at Nature's door,

*

Sun Reflects

Sun reflects on green leaves.
Reminds me Spring is here.
What eggs the seasonal bird conceives
Will, doubtless, soon appear,
And all the seeds
The new nest needs
Will fill the mother's craw,
While the father drives his foes away,
Lest eggs become their cowardly prey
Before the how of birth arrives.
And so, each year is like the last
And life gives future to the past.

*

The Bridge

We need to build a bridge to join us.
We seem to be existing far apart.
This loneliness is sure to ruin us
In mind, in spirit and in heart.
It's not about the time and distance.
I know we're bound in some great way.
It's more about our own resistance
To what we choose to do or what we say.
There is a fear-based vacuum between us
Which only love and compassion can fill.
Acts of kindness promise to redeem us,
And surely, by the Grace of God, they will.
My friend, walk with me in understanding.
Our paths, no doubt, will finally cross.
Acceptance overcomes selfish demanding,
As service makes us happier than being the boss.
This is a bridge we build of common glue

Across a chasm made of nothingness.
I can never walk your passage for you,
But I will help you overcome distress.
I can be still and listen to you.
May God be merciful and heaven bless.

*

The Spring Has Come

The Spring has come upon the land
and blossoms fill the trees.
The birds in song
fly swiftly on,
flight aided by the breeze.
But all the blessings in the land
amount to little more
than omens come
to beat the drum
rejoicing at your door.
For you were born, the Spring at hand,
to create love in all our land.

*

Thoughts

The thoughts are there,
But the feelings dwell in deep despair,
So the thoughts form words that go nowhere.
I cannot write what I feel is wrong.
I will not sing a negative song.
So, I spend my time
In hapless rhyme
In the pretense that I don't care.

*

Walking through Woods

Walking through woods is humbling.
The trees seem to mark the passing of another creature.
The branches wave and the leaves whisper.
When the lichen notes the creature's age,
A slight chuckle might be imagined,
As one might offer when contemplating a grandchild.
I was born in Oregon, not far from Bandon By The Sea.
I return there, occasionally,
To refresh my self-awareness,
As I am given to egotism
And my conference with the trees
Renews my sense of belonging
To both the present
And the myriad histories
In which this land glories.
I recall Johnny Appleseed,
Paul Bunyan and other
Mystical personalities.
These many-ringed personages

Seem to help me understand.
Then, I walk to the shore
And listen to the roar
Of the waves upon the sand.

*

We Are Free

Always, there will be injustice,
Born of fear - born in prejudice
And jealousy. But we need not be
The servants of these fears,
Nor the bearers of their injustices.
We are free to rise above them
And embrace our dreams -
Free to share our love with all
Whom we meet on the path we walk.

*

We Walk Along

We walk along a myriad paths,
Enroute to who knows where.
We see and hear.
We taste.
We smell.
We touch the ground we walk upon
And feel the wind in our hair.
But, what we're thinking,
none can tell
Unless we deem it wise to speak
Or, in display, convey emotion.
Otherwise, our secret thoughts
Are like small waves
upon the ocean,
And what we have to share
May as well not be there.

*

What's Right

As shadows drift across the day
And secrets find the light,
Our hope rests in the simple way
We try to do what's right.
No promise holds us in contempt.
We act as though new born.
Though worldly cares may tease and tempt,
We look on them with scorn.
For we have found a treasure trove
Too real to be ignored.
Based in humility and love,
It lives, our eternal reward.

*

When We Give Words

When we give words to anger,
We give power to fear,
Not in those whom we resent,
But within ourselves.
When we speak forgiveness,
And see flaws in others
For what they really are,
Human frailty,
And we recognize
Those flaws in ourselves.
Then we are given the power
To correct ourselves,
That others may benefit.

*

Prism

Do not believe that this limited perspective
Is the only view available to you and me,
Or by which we can truly see,
For light is refracted with infinite possibility.
Our fixed and proven tenets are, in fact,
But walls we've built to keep our fears intact.
Should we allow the light to shine anew
From an altered and distorted point of view,
We may discover many another
Acceptable understanding
Of our place in this temporal world
On which our vulnerable minds are landing.

*

Printed in the United States
by Baker & Taylor Publisher Services